CONFLICT RESC
RELATIONS

EFFECTIVE
COMMUNICATION
FOR COUPLES

101 Proven Strategies To Be In Complete Harmony With Your Partner

Lela Payne

Table of Contents

Chapter 1:

24 Tips For Conflict Resolution In Relationships

It's normal to have conflict in relationships. People are different, and their desires and needs will inevitably clash. Resolving disagreements in a healthy way creates understanding and brings couples closer together. The objective should be the betterment of the relationship. This is positive conflict. Below are 24 suggested rules for actualizing this goal.

The Role of Self-Esteem

Self-esteem is essential to assertiveness and healthy communication, which lay the foundation for avoiding fights and handling conflict. Unfortunately, this isn't the norm, especially among co-dependent couples. Not having had good role models for expressing anger and handling conflict, one or both partners is usually passive or aggressive.

When it comes to disagreements, low self-esteem leads to:

- Taking things personally

- Defensiveness

- Inability to express needs and wants

- High reactivity

- People-pleasing

- Not taking responsibility for behaviour, feelings, and needs

- Inability to be honest

- Undisclosed expectations of others

Rules of Engagement

In positive conflict, ideally, you're able to verbalize your needs and wants and mutually work out compromises. Your intent and how you approach differences are critical. The objective should be to resolve a dispute to the satisfaction of both of you. It's not about winning and losing. You can "win" an argument, but the relationship may suffer if your partner feels discounted, deflated, or resentful.

Planning when, where, and how you approach a disagreement is important for achieving satisfactory results. It's helpful make up rules of engagement in advance. Here are suggested 12 Do's and 12 Don't's. You won't be able to achieve all of them or any all the time, but they're guidelines to strive for:

DO:

1. Make it okay to "agree to disagree." You don't have to agree on everything. Try to accept irresolvable differences that don't violate your values.

2. Have time-limited discussions and stick to the pre-set time. A half-hour is plenty. You can always reconvene.

3. Work through things as they come up. Don't stockpile resentments; otherwise, each postponement becomes a block to the next communication.

4. Remember to maintain goodwill by separating the person you care about from the behavior. Assume he or she is doing their best and isn't hurting you intentionally.

5. Take responsibility for your behavior, needs, and feelings. Use "I" statements to share your feelings and thoughts about yourself. This doesn't include "I feel you're inconsiderate." Instead, say "I feel unimportant to you."

6. Examine what unmet needs are making you angry. With I statements, be direct and honest about your feelings and needs in the relationship. Communicate the positive consequences of compliance.

7. Listen with curiosity and a desire to understand your partner, and to see the world through his or her eyes. When you don't understand, ask for clarification. Remember that your partner is telling you his or her experience. It reveals the truth about them, not you. You're free to disagree, but first see where the person is coming from.

8. Use a "we" approach. "We have a problem," not "My problem with you is . . ."

9. Rather than demand your way, brainstorm solutions. Request your partner's input, especially when it comes to changing his or her behaviour.

10. Take a time-out if you start to get angry. This allows you to calm down and stop reacting. Reassure your partner that you'll resume.

11. Use breaks to take responsibility for your part, think about solutions, and to self-soothe any hurt feelings.

12. Communicate your fears and guilt in the relationship.

DON'T:

1. Don't have controversial discussions when you're tired or the bedroom, which should kept a safe place.

2. Don't make accusations or use the words, "always" or "never."

3. Don't bring in allies – other people's opinions – or make comparisons to others.

4. Don't switch topics, or retaliate with, "but you did . . ."

5. Don't judge, blame, belittle, or be sarcastic or dismissive in words or facial expressions, such as rolling your eyes or smirking.

6. Don't expect your partner to read your mind.

7. Don't analyse your partner or impute motives or feelings to him or her.

8. Don't interrupt or monopolize the conversation.

9. Don't react or defend yourself. Instead communicate your point of view.

10. Don't bring up the past – anything more than a few days old.

11. Don't rolodex grievances. Stick to the current one. You don't need more "evidence" that you're right and your partner is wrong.

12. Don't compromise your bottom lines in the relationship, if they're non-negotiable. It will lead to more conflict later.

Chapter 2:

6 Important Conversation For Couples To Have

How many kids you want, how often you floss, what flavour wedding cake you're imagining — these topics aren't exactly appropriate for first-date conversations. But by the time you're in a serious relationship, there are certain subjects you absolutely must discuss if you're going to continue to build a healthy partnership.

So, whether you're already hitched, thinking about shacking up, or even if you've been dating for years without any intention of moving in together or getting married, this list is for you. Check out the six discussions you and your partner need to have, STAT.

1. The Dolla-Dolla Bills Discussion

Even if you've never explicitly talked about money, you probably already have a vague idea of how much your partner makes and how he/she likes to spend a paycheck. Still, if there's a possibility that you two might end up sharing a bank account or co-owning a house (or if you already are), it's crucial to have a conversation about finances. Taffy Wagner, financial expert and CEO of MoneyTalkMatters.com, told Woman's Day that one important question to ask your partner is, "How did you manage your money when you were on your own?" It's also a good idea, Wagner said, to decide which partner will be the main financial manager (although he/she always needs to keep the other partner informed).

2. The Communication Conversation

Wait — why would you talk about fighting if you're not actually mad at each other? Because learning about your partner's communication style, especially when he/she wants to talk about something that's bothersome, helps prevent big blow-ups down the road. Relationship expert Rebecca Hendrix writes on TheKnot.com that it's useful to think back to a recent quarrel and analyze it to see how each partner approached the situation differently. It could be that you chose to speak up the minute your partner did something annoying. It could be that your partner needs some time to process his/her emotions before beginning a discussion. Just knowing this information is really valuable for handling future conflicts.

3. The Fuss About The Future

For sure, thinking about what lies ahead for you two can be seriously anxiety provoking. While it might be nicer to just lay in bed together binge-watching Modern Family and "enjoy the moment," a serious relationship requires some conversation about what each person envisions for the next few years. Are you planning to apply to Ph.D.

programs all over the country? Is your partner hoping to quit his/her job and travel for a year? As Dr. Laura Berman, a sex and relationship educator and therapist, writes on Everyday Health, it's important to get on the same page about your plans. Make sure to cover all the possibilities now so that, should one of them become a reality, you'll be as prepared as possible.

4. The Cinderella Story

Unfortunately, this conversation is less about romance and Prince Charming and more about household chores. Especially for couples who live together, it's important to figure out who's responsible for and actually enjoys which everyday tasks. According to relationship expert Paulette Kouffman-Sherman, the most important thing is that the division of chores feels fair. So if you hate cooking, go ahead and ask your partner if he/she would prefer to take charge in the kitchen, while you agree to wash the dishes afterward.

5. The Cheating Chat

Sometimes infidelity is easily defined. Having sex with someone else in the bed you share with your partner? Ding, ding, ding! That is cheating, times a thousand. But don't take your partner's thoughts about infidelity for granted. It's worth having a sit-down discussion about what exactly constitutes cheating in the context of your unique relationship. Online communication is especially tricky — Dr. Aaron Ben-Zeev writes on

PsychologyToday.com that people have different ideas about whether a virtual connection is actually an instance of infidelity if there's no in-person interaction. There are all kinds of relationships with all kinds of boundaries, so make sure to figure out what yours are before someone gets hurt.

6. The "Tell Me About Your Childhood" Exchange

I know, I know. "Love is blind" and all that. The truth is, you can totally love someone from a different cultural or religious background, but that doesn't mean your different upbringings won't prove challenging at times. In fact, even if you two are from nearly identical backgrounds, you can still have developed different <u>cultural and religious values</u>. When a relationship starts to get serious, therapists at the University of Texas say it's a good idea to <u>talk about your values</u> — how often you typically attend religious services (if at all), which holidays are most important for you to celebrate (if any), etc.

Chapter 3:

6 Ways To Deal With Gaslighting In A Relationship

We call it gas lighting when someone manipulates you into thinking that you are confused about your feelings or when someone makes you doubt them. It is crucial to know if you are gaslit in a relationship to break that chain of toxicity. It leaves you with doubts as well as insecurities within yourself. So good to end it as soon as possible. People gaslight others to make sure that you do what they want. You will notice that gradually you do things that they would like you to do. They manipulate you into doing what they like.

People who gaslight others in a relationship trivialize their feelings. They will address your even tiniest of feelings as overreacting. They try to control the situation their way. Changing details about something that happened in the past and constantly blames you for everything they did. When it comes to your needs or wants, they frequently change the subject, ensuring that you always think about what they would like or want. They keep you low on the priority list while they keep themselves upon yours. All we need is to be safe from these kinds of people. For that, the following are the ways to deal with gaslighting.

1. Confirm Manipulation

People may confuse someone's rude behavior or childish behavior with gaslighting. It's not always necessarily true that the other person is gaslighting. It might be their true nature to talk with an attitude. It is commonly mistaken for gaslighting in a relationship. Gaslighting is the repetitive behavior of deceiving or manipulation the same person. If the person is not polite towards you, then it may not be considered manipulation in any way. People may gaslight you unintentionally too. When they say something in the heat of the moment, it doesn't necessarily mean they want to manipulate you.

2. Speak Up

When you stay quiet in times of raising your voice, then it becomes a habit. When they know that you won't speak up to them about their behavior, they burden you more. You get habitual of not speaking back, and they get habitual of getting away with manipulation or lies every time. Show them that you won't accept the way they treat you. They will eventually find their mistake or find out that it was not worth it.

3. Stay Self-Assured

When a manipulative person tries to change the small details about any event, you need to be confident in your version of the story you think happened. When they see you constantly hesitating, then they become more confident in their version. They will start making you doubt yourself in a way that whatever they say sounds true. You need to be firm on your point and make them see that you know the truth of the situation.

4. Self-Aid

No matter what you think is vital in your life, it would be best if you were your priority, always. Self-aid or self-care is extremely important for a person to follow with or without a relationship. A gaslighting person will always try to make themselves your priority. In that case, you need to stand your ground and show them that you come first in every aspect of your life. With self-care, you will be active mentally and physically. You will get the power to fight for yourself.

5. Communicate With Friends

It's more reliable to talk to others about your situation. When you are confused about your partner's behavior, you can always ask for support from someone you trust. They will help you get a better idea of the situation you are in and maybe help you get out of it. Third-party who knows both sides of the story will help you sort out your relationship.

6. Administrative Support

It is always helpful to seek professional knowledge from people as they know much better than us and understand the situation much more clearly. Ask them for help. They will professionally help you out and make sure you are okay. Gaslighting is not to be taken lightly. Professional service will always be available for those who feel like reaching out for it. There is no embarrassment in seeking executive help.

Conclusion

There are lots of people who are suffering from gaslighting. If you think that you are one of them, then you need to follow each step carefully. Make sure that you feel safe and sound in your life. The person gaslighting will eventually make their mistake but don't wait for them too. Get out of that toxic relationship as soon as possible.

Chapter 4:

Dealing With Abuse In Relationship

Why can't they simply leave the relationship? This is one question that people frequently ask when they see someone is being abused in a relationship. But if you are the one who is in an abusive relationship, you will know that it not this easy. Ending a relationship that means a lot to you is never easy to end. It gets even more difficult when you have been psychologically beaten down, physically threatened, isolated from your friends and family, and financially controlled. If you are in an abusive relationship and want to leave, you might be feeling torn or confused—one moment you want to leave, the other you want to stay. You might even blame yourself for the abuse. If you are in an abusive relationship, we want you to remember;

- You are not to blame for being battered or mistreated.

- You deserve a safe and happy life.

- You are not the cause of your partner's abusive behavior.

- You are not alone. People are waiting to help.

- You deserve to be treated with respect.

- Your children deserve a safe and happy life.

Now, when you have to decide whether to stay in a relationship or to leave, here are some of the things you should keep in mind:

If You're Hoping Abusive Partners Will Change

That is probably not going to happen; these people have deep psychological and emotional issues; although change is not something that is impossible but is not easy or quick, and change is only possible if the abuser takes full responsibility for their behavior.

Suppose You Believe You Can Help Your Abuser

In that case, that is a natural phenomenon you will that you are the only one who understands them or that it is your responsibility to fix their problems. Still, the actual truth is that when you stay, you accept constant abuse, and you enable them, so instead of helping them, you are perpetuating the problem.

Suppose Your Partner Has Promised To Stop The Abuse

In that case, that is probably what they say at the moment because when they face, the consequences they plead for another chance and promise to change or beg for forgiveness. They might even mean it at the moment, but their actual goal is to stay in control and keep you from leaving them, and as soon as you will forgive them, they will return to their abusive behavior as soon as you forgive them because they are no longer worried that you will leave them.

Even If your partner is in counseling, there is no guarantee that they will change; there are many abusers that go through and continue to be violent, aggressive, controlling, and abusive. Suppose your partner has stopped making excuses and is showing visible signs of change, then that is good. However, you should decide based on who they are right now, not on the hope of who they would become.

If you are worried about what will happen once you leave, it is valid to be afraid of your abusive partner's will and where you will go, or how you will support your children or yourself. But you should not let this fear of the unknown keep you in an abusive relationship.

Here are some signs that your abuser is not changing.

- They minimize the abuse or denies how serious it was.
- They pressurize you to make decisions about the relationship.
- They say that they can't change unless you stay with him and support him.
- You have to push him to stay in treatment.
- They tell you that you owe him another chance.

- They try to get sympathy from you, your children, or your family and friends.

- They claim that you're the abusive one.

- They pressure you to go to couple's counseling.

- They expect something from you in exchange for getting help.

- They continue to blame others for his behavior.

Chapter 5:

7 Ways To Forgive You Partner

Forgiveness usually means to stop being angry or to stop blaming someone who made a mistake. Forgive and let go of it hurts a lot in a relationship, but it is also essential to keep it happy and healthy.

1. Take Your time To Forgive

Ask your partner to give you some space. You were able to forgive needs some time. It involves patience and trust. Sit alone and think about it. Think about how and why you are going to forgive your partner. Make up your mind for everything. Make your mind up for any further challenges or consequences. Think about how you are going to tell him what's in your mind and heart. If you can't think alone, ask a friend for advice. Get consultation if needed.

2. Forgiveness Helps You Heal

Holding onto resentment can sour you and keep you from finding peace. When you can't forgive, your emotional wounds can't close and heal. Forgiveness allows you to let go of pain and continue with a lighter heart.

Forgiveness, in other words, enables you to begin moving away from anger and resentment before they seep into all areas of your life.

3. Talk When You Are Ready

Honest communication is vital at this juncture. Sit together. Tell your partner what's been on your mind. Let them know how you feel and how much it has affected you. Tell them that the word forgive means that the person who did something will never do this again. If they agree that what they did will never do it again will then be ignored. Also, ask your partner what they are feeling and how they are coping with this situation. Ask them how they want this relationship to be healthy. You can't truly forgive without empathy and compassion. Committing to forgiveness is only the beginning, and memories of your hurt may still resurface after you've decided to ignore it. Holding on to understanding and patience can help you succeed.

4. Forgive But Don't Forget

Forgiving your partner for what they did is a crucial step, and forgiving can achieve it, but forgetting is the hard part. It is not like you should forget what happened, but forgetting can be attained by redefining boundaries in a way that will let your relationship move past a setback and start a new chapter. Rebuilding trust essentially happens through actions, not words.

5. Forgiveness Helps You Reconcile

You can forgive someone even if you know you can never have the same relationship. Depending on the circumstances, you may even need to avoid contact. That said, everyone makes mistakes. When a loved one hurts you, forgiving them can open the door to relationship repair. In many cases, the act of forgiveness can help someone who inadvertently caused pain to realize how they hurt you. This provides an opportunity for learning and growth. Forgiveness may not mend your relationship immediately, but it's a good start.

6. Find The Bright Side

When someone hurts you, you're probably not in a position to notice any benefits that came out of the situation. In time, you may have more emotional space to recognize what you've gained. Even when you can't identify a clear benefit, you may feel like a better person for embracing compassion and understanding.

7. Try To Move On

You can't ignore the challenges life throws at you. But prioritizing compassion and empathy can make it easier to notice the good things and give them more weight than the bad. If something positive did come out of it, you already have some practice finding the flower amongst the rubble. You don't have to believe that everything has meaning or happens because of destiny. You can make your meaning and find your good, no matter what life brings.

Conclusion

It's normal to want someone to regret the pain they inflicted. The truth is, this doesn't always happen. Some people aren't capable of recognizing when they cause pain. Others don't see their mistakes or don't care. You may never get an explanation or an apology. Letting bitterness and resentment maintain a hold over you only gives them power. Instead of letting the past hold you back, use what you learned from the experience to take steps to protect yourself from future pain.

Chapter 6:

6 Ways On How To Make Your Partner Feel Loved

The word partner has a deep meaning. It means the association with each other. They understand each other, respecting and supporting every step and decision of each other. In simple words, a partner indicates being fully committed to each other.

Being committed includes many challenges, but one of the biggest and the main challenges is how to make your partner feel loved. This is a big challenge because many partners still don't understand each other entirely after spending most of the time together. Efforts from both partners can help in this situation which can lead to a happy and healthy relationship.

Comforting each other in every situation, mostly in their challenging times, has always played a key role in making your partner feel loved. Your partner knows that you are always there to support them and expressing your willingness to make them relieved, and never doubt their decision.

1. Complementing Each Other

Many people think that the female partner in a relationship needs compliments, but the truth is every human being on this planet needs compliments sometimes. Compliments matter a lot, even for boys, but they don't show that they need compliments. Even if they are complimented, they don't show the happiness of being praised. Being praised by a stranger or not so close doesn't matter a lot, but if the compliment comes from an immediate or loved one, it means the world to them. Complimenting each other back and forth can also improve communication, which is the building block.

2. Be Attentive Towards Each Other

Taking each other for granted destroys a relationship. Instead, try to give all of your attention to your partner. It strengthens a connection. It makes them feel wanted. Listen to them with your complete attention. Listen to the first and then give your opinion or comfort them depending on the situation. Pay him the attention the partner deserves because every moment you spend with him is crucial. Whether planning a dinner or a movie night, always carve out time to be with each other. And when you're spending that quality time together, let things flow naturally and give your partner your undivided attention. Show your interest in them and make them feel that you want to be in their company.

3. Little Gestures of Love

Little gestures can also show your partner how much you care about them and make them feel special and loved. Small gestures can include checking on them, texting them, calling them to say how much you miss them, making plans to meet them, sending small meaningful gifts, asking how their day was and what they are doing tomorrow. Plan surprises for them. Randomly say how much you love them. These small gestures will make their day a hundred percent better.

4. Accept That

Acknowledge your partner. Appreciate them for what they are doing for you. Thank them for their attention and their support, and the love they have given. Thank them just for being there. No one is perfect. Everyone has flaws, and those flaws need to be accepted. A person can never be in front of the person they love until and unless the person they love accepts for who they are and accepts their flaws.

5. Appreciate Them

Make them feel special. Make them feel proud of who you have chosen as a partner. Tell them that it was the right decision to choose them as a partner. Send them appreciation paragraphs. Tell them that they are important and they matter and that you cannot take a step or decision without their opinion. Relive and remember your memories with them.

Take a trip down memory lane once in a while. Cherish your happy memories, remember you are bad ones too, and promise each other that no more memories like these will ever be made again. Try not to break promises. Try to fulfill them.

6. Excite Each Other Up

Compliment his accomplishments. Tell him that you are proud of what he accomplished and how hard he worked for those accomplishments. Tell him how he deserved what he accomplished.

Conclusion

Be abundant with happiness. Let your partner lead. Respect him. Be loyal and faithful and give your hundred percent. Be kind and forgive them. Never let your ego win, and never let pride enter your heart.

Chapter 7:

Ten Ways Men Fall In Love

Genuine and true Love is so rare that when you encounter it in any form, it's a beautiful thing to be utterly cherished in whatever form it takes. But how does one get this genuine and true Love? Almost every romantic movie, we have seen that a guy meets a girl and, sure enough, falls head over heels for her. But translating that into the real world can be quite a task. The science of attraction works wonders for us. Sometimes we are instantly drawn to some people. On the other hand, we couldn't care less for others. And quite a few times, things flow naturally in our direction, making it all feel surreal and causing butterflies.

A famous psychologist once said: "Love is about an expansion of the self whereby another person's interests, values, social network, and finances become part of your life just as you share your resources with them."

A human mind is, nonetheless, a very complex organ. It can either makes you feel like you're on top of the world with its positive attitude or under it with its negative one. And a male mind, perhaps, seems always like a mystery to us. But it's not such rocket science that we can't get our hands on it. If you're developing feelings for someone and need a bit of guidance to get the man of your dreams to notice you and care about you, then you've just come to the right place!

Here are some ways about what a man needs to fall in Love.

1. Always Be Yourself

Keeping a façade of fake personality and pretending to be someone you're not can be a huge turn-off for men. Instead let the guy know the real you. Let them see who you really are and what you really have to offer. You will not only gain respect from them, but you wouldn't have to keep hiding behind a mask. If you're pretending to be someone else, that only suggests that you're not comfortable with yourself. And many guys will realize this shortcoming and quickly become disinterested. You don't have to dumb down your intellect or put a damper on your exuberant personality. Men like women who are completely honest with them from the start. Who shows them their vulnerable side as well as their opinionated and intelligent one. You're in no need to pretend that your IQ isn't off the charts. Be your genuine, miserable, confident, and independent self always. That way, he will know exactly what he's getting into.

2. Make Him Feel Accepted And Appreciated

From a simple thank you text to calling him and asking him about his day, making small gestures for him, and complimenting and praising him, a man needs it all. Men don't always show it, but they are loved to be told that they look good, they're doing a good job, or how intellectual they are. Sometimes men are confused about where women may stand, and they want to see that he's being supported beyond any superficial matter. When men share glimpses of their inner self with you and put themselves in a vulnerable position, which men rarely do, this is when it's crucial to make him feel rest assured that he will be accepted and appreciated. If women make men feel lifted high and admired, then it's pure magic for them. His heart will make such a deep connection with you that it can only be amplified from thereon.

3. Listen! Don't Just Talk

You would see a lot of men complain that they are not heard enough. And quite frankly, it is true. It's essential to establish a mutual balance in the conversation. Women shouldn't make it all about themselves. They need to let the men speak and hear them attentively, and respond accordingly. Ask him questions about his life and his passion, his likes and dislikes. That way, he'll know that you are genuinely interested in him. Men have a lot to say when you show that you can listen. They'll be more inclined to say the things that matter.

4. Laugh Out Loud With Him

Men tend to make the women of their liking laugh a lot. When you're laughing, you're setting off chemicals in a guy's brain to feel good. Make him feel like he has a great sense of humor, and he's making you happy with his silly and jolly mannerism. Similarly, men are attracted to women who have a spirit that can make them feel good. Tell him enjoyable stories, roast people with him, jump in on his jokes and laugh wholeheartedly with him. He will become attracted to you.

5. Look Your Best

You don't have to shred a few pounds, or get clear, glowing skin, or change your hairstyle to impress the men of your liking. You have to be confident enough in your skin! Men love a confident woman who feels secure about herself and her appearance. You don't even have to wear body-hugging clothes or tight jeans to make him drool over you (Of course, you can wear them if you want). But a simple pair of jeans and a t-shirt can go a long way too. Just remember to clean yourself up nice, put on nice simple clothes, wear that unique perfume, style up your hair a bit, and voila! You're good to go.

6. Be Trustworthy

Another reason that men instantly attract you is when they have the surety that they can trust you with anything and everything. According to love and marriage experts "Trust is not something all loving relationships start with, but successful marriages and relationships thrive on it. Trust is so pervasive that it becomes part of the fabric of these strong relationship." If you want to win a man's heart, reassure him that he can be vulnerable around you and make him feel accepted and secure.

7. Don't Try To Change Him

"He's completely right for me... if only he didn't dress up like that or snore during his sleep."

Sure we might have a few things on our list about how our partner should be, but that doesn't mean we should forcibly try to change their habits. He might have a few annoying habits that will get on your nerves now and then, but that shouldn't be a dealbreaker for you. Instead, we should accept him with all his wits and flaws. You shouldn't just tolerate his little quirks but rather try to admire them too. If something about him is bothering you, try talking to him politely about it. And he might consider changing it for you!

8. Have Intellectual Conversations With Him:

There's nothing that a man finds sexier than women with opinion and intellect. Get his views on a news article, engage him in a heated debate about controversial topics, put your views out the front; even if they clash with his, especially if they conflict with his, he'd be more interested and intrigued about knowing your stance. Show your future partner that you can carry on an intelligent conversation with him anytime he likes.

9. Be Patient:

I can't stress enough that patience is perhaps the most vital key to getting a guy to fall for you. It would be best if you gave him time to analyze and process his feelings for you. If you tend to rush him on the subject, you might end up disappointed. Even if you do lose your cool, don't let him know it. Just be patient and consistent, and don't come off as too clingy or needy. If you appear too desperate, it's going to turn him off of the relationship entirely.

10. Let Him Know You're Thinking Of Him

In the early days of dating, you might be hesitant to tell him that you're thinking of him. You love it when he texts you randomly, saying he's thinking about you, so why not reciprocate it? Invest your time, energy, and efforts in him. Leave him short, sweet notes, or text him in the middle of the day saying that he is on your mind or sending him a greeting card with a cute personal message. Don't overdo it by reminding him constantly if he does not respond. None of these screams' overboard' and are guaranteed to make him smile.

Conclusion

I hope this article deconstructed and gave you some insights into what makes a man fall for a woman. As the saying goes, 'Men are from mars and women are from Venus and Venus is great, but surely, we need to know about the inner workings of mars too.' Just keep the above tips in mind, be consistent and commit to him considerably, and you're good to go! If you found this video helpful, don't forget to like, subscribe, comment, and share this with someone important to you. I hope you learned something valuable today. Take care, have a good rest, and till the next video ☺

Chapter 8:

10 Ways To Attract Love

The following ideas are to attract **true love** and romance into your life. These fun and practical little tips will magnify your energy and get the Law of Attraction sending more love your way whether you're single or need a little spark in your relationship.

1. Get Specific: What Kind Of A Relationship Would You Like In Your Life?

Take out a piece of paper or open up a document on your computer and list out what kind of relationship you would like to have in your life. What does it look like? How does it work? Will you get married? Get specific. God/The Universe/Source Energy is always in the details.

2. Let Go Of Your Past, De-Clutter And Move Forward

This means not talking about 'him or her' as much and perhaps getting rid of old love letters or emails that keep you stuck in the past. It's time to pave the way for a new person to step forward. They can't arrive when you're still pining over someone else.

3. Watch Movies Of The Love You Would Like To Attract

Without a doubt 'The Notebook' is the romantic movie that most people refer to when they think of the type of love they would like to attract. Go to IMDB and search for romantic movies and create a 'must watch list'.

4. Show Yourself The Love You Think You Deserve

It's really important to know how good (or not so good) your levels of self-esteem are. You really need to love yourself in order to attract a relationship that is sustainable. The truth? Otherwise you'll be attracting someone that will want to fix you or will magnify your need to take care of yourself better. This can be a good thing, but unless you shine light on the need for self-love and self-care then it can turn ugly very fast. So this is why it's so important to treat yourself well and show yourself the love you think you deserve. How will you love yourself today? Ask yourself this powerful question at least 3 times per day.

5. Buy Yourself Flowers Or Tickets To Something You Want To Watch

Surrounding yourself with bunches of fresh and beautiful blooms is a great way to raise your vibration. It encapsulates the essence of springtime and is really lovely and feminine. Also take yourself on a date to the movies. Watch something that you really want to see. This is an act of strengthening levels of self love.

6. Create Space In Your Bedroom For Your Lover

I learnt this one from 'The Game of Life and How to Play It' where Florence Scovel Shinn writes about the importance of demonstrating something called 'active faith'. It's where you create space for whatever it is that you wish to welcome in your life. By creating space in your bedroom for your lover you are letting the Universe know that you're ready. You can do this by just sleeping on one side of the bed, making drawer space available for his or her clothes.

7. Soul Mate Journal Exercise

Write a clear list of all of the things you would like to do with your soul mate. List out the dates, tourist attractions, events and fun things you can do together. Feel excited about sharing these experiences with someone.

8. Crystal Magic

Get some rose quartz to flow energy into and use it as an attraction point for manifesting love. Carry it with you as a reminder of the lover that is on track to find you soon.

9. Buy A Special Dinner Plate For Your Lover Or A Coffee Cup

Imagine making a cup of tea or coffee for your lover each morning. By buying a special cup you can visualize the process of having him/her there with you. The Universe will respond to this action.

10. Feel Energized When You See Others In Love

Don't be one of those people that see public displays of affection or people blissfully in love and allow it to activate your crabby/skeptical mind. You can only attract success when you are genuinely happy for others and their success. Allow yourself to be energized by the love that others share and affirm to yourself that your time is on its way very soon.

Chapter 9:

6 Signs You Are Emotionally Unavailable

In times of need, all we want is emotional comfort. The people around us mainly provide it. But the question is, will we support them if the need arises? You might be emotionally unavailable for them when they need you. It is necessary to have some emotional stability to form some strong bonds. If you are emotionally unapproachable, you will have fewer friends than someone you stand mentally tall. It is not harmful to be emotionally unavailable, but you need to change that in the long run. And for that, you need to reflect on yourself first.

It would help if you always were your top priority. While knowing why you are emotionally unapproachable, you need to focus on yourself calmly. Giving respect and talking is not enough for someone to rely on you. You need to support them whenever needed. Talk your mind with them. Be honest with them. But not in a rude way, in a comforting way. So, next time they will come to you for emotional support and comfort. If you are relating to all these things, then here are some signs that confirm it.

1. You Keep People At A Distance

It is usual for an emotionally unavailable person to be seen alone at times. They tend to stay aloof at times; that way, they don't have to be emotionally available. And even if you meet people, you always find it challenging to make a bond with them. You might have a few friends and family members close to you. But you always find meeting new people an emotionally draining activity. You also might like to hang out with people, but opening up is not your forte. If you are emotionally unavailable, then you keep people at a hands distance from you.

2. You Have Insecurities

If you struggle to love yourself, then count it as a sign of emotional stress. People are likely to be unavailable emotionally for others when they are emotionally unavailable for themselves too. We always doubt the people who love us. How can they when I, myself, can't? And this self-hatred eventually results in a distant relationship with your fellow beings. Pampering yourself time by time is essential for every single one of us. It teaches us how one should be taken care of and how to support each other.

3. You Have A Terrible Past Experience

This could be one of the reasons for your unapproachable nature towards people. When you keep some terrible memory or trauma stored inside of you, it's most likely you cannot comfort some other being. It won't seem like something you would do. Because you keep this emotional difference, you become distant and are forced to live with those memories, making things worse. It would help if you talked things out. Either your parents or your friends. Tell them whatever is on your mind, and you will feel light at heart. Nothing can change the past once it's gone, but we can work on the future.

4. You Got Heartbroken

In most cases, people are not born with this nature to be emotionally unavailable. It often comes with heartbreak. If you had a breakup with your partner, that could affect your emotional life significantly. And if it was a long-term relationship, then you got emotionally deprived. But on the plus side, you got single again. Ready to choose from scratch. Instead, you look towards all the negative points of this breakup. Who knows, maybe you'll find someone better.

5. You Are An Introvert

Do you hate going to parties or gatherings? Does meeting with friends sound tiresome? If yes, then surprise, you are an introvert. Social life can be a mess sometimes. Sometimes we prefer a book to a person. That trait of ours makes us emotionally unavailable for others. It is not a bad thing to stay at home on a Friday night, but going out once in a while may be healthy for you. And the easiest way to do that is to make an extrovert friend. Then you won't need to make an effort. Everything will go smoothly.

6. You Hate Asking For Help

Do you feel so independent that you hate asking for help from others? Sometimes when we get support from others, we feel like they did a favor for us. So, instead of asking for help, we prefer to do everything alone, by ourselves. Asking for aid, from superior or inferior, is no big deal. Everyone needs help sometimes.

Conclusion

Being emotionally unavailable doesn't make you a wrong person but being there for others gives us self-comfort too. It's not all bad to interact with others; instead, it's pretty fun if you try. It will make your life much easier, and you will have a lot of support too.

Chapter 10:

What Is The Meaning of Life?

The question of the meaning of life is perhaps one that we would rather not ask, for <u>fear</u> of the answer or lack thereof. Still today, many people believe that we, humankind, are the creation of a supernatural entity called God, that God had an intelligent purpose in creating us, and that this intelligent purpose is "the meaning of life".

I do not propose to rehearse the well-worn arguments for and against the existence of God, and still less to take a side. But even if God exists, and even if He had an intelligent purpose in creating us, no one really knows what this purpose might be, or that it is especially meaningful. The Second Law of Thermodynamics states that the entropy of a closed system—including the universe itself—increases up to the point at which equilibrium is reached, and God's purpose in creating us, and, indeed, all of nature, might have been no more lofty than to catalyse this process much as soil organisms catalyse the decomposition of organic matter.

If our God-given purpose is to act as super-efficient heat dissipators, then having no purpose at all is better than having this sort of purpose—because it frees us to be the authors of our purpose or purposes and so to lead truly dignified and meaningful lives. In fact, following this logic, having no purpose at all is better than having any kind of pre-determined purpose, even more traditional, uplifting ones such as serving God or improving our karma.

In short, even if God exists, and even if He had an intelligent purpose in creating us (and why should He have had?), we do not know what this purpose might be, and, whatever it might be, we would rather be able to do without it, or at least to ignore or discount it. For unless we can be free to become the authors of our own purpose or purposes, our lives may have, at worst, no purpose at all, and, at best, only some unfathomable and potentially trivial purpose that is not of our own choosing.

You might yet object that talk about the meaning of life is neither here nor there because life is merely a prelude to some form of eternal afterlife, and this, if you will, is its purpose. But I can marshal up at least four arguments against this position:

- It is not at all clear that there is, or even can be, some form of eternal afterlife that entails the survival of the personal ego.

- Even if there were such an afterlife, living for ever is not in itself a purpose. The concept of the afterlife merely displaces the problem to one remove, begging the question: what then is the purpose of the afterlife? If the afterlife has a pre-determined purpose, again, we do not know what that is, and, whatever it is, we would rather be able to do without it.

- Reliance on an eternal afterlife not only postpones the question of life's purpose, but also dissuades or at least discourages us from determining a purpose or purposes for what may be the only life that we do have.

Chapter 11:

8 Signs Someone Misses You

Missing someone can be very painful, almost as if there is something incomplete about your life. You think about them all the time, and the more you try not to think of them, the more you end up doing that. You might find your thoughts wandering and can't seem to focus on anything other than them. You may either find comfort in binge eating or constantly go through their stuff. Well, you're not the only one who might be going through this torture. What if someone is experiencing the same stuff but for you? Here are some signs that tell you someone is missing you.

1. They Keep Track Of Your Social Media:

If they haven't unfriended, unfollowed, or blocked you yet, the chances are that they are still keeping track of you. If you find them constantly reacting to your stories, or liking your pictures the minute you put them up, then they're visiting your profile again and again. They have kept their slot open for making a conversation or giving you a hint to try to make conversation with them.

2. Did They Find Your Replacement Yet?

For someone ready to move on, it takes a second to find a replacement. If they haven't found one yet, the chances are that they are still reminiscing over you. They're hoping that you'll reconnect and thus, still pine after you. Even if they're hooking up with someone as a rebound, chances are they're doing everything in their power to forget you but are failing miserably.

3. They Reach Out To You Randomly

Receiving those drunk late-night texts/calls? They're miserable, and all they want to do is talk to you. If they were out there having the time of their life, they wouldn't even remember you let alone bother to text or call you. If they do, it's obviously because you're on their mind and alcohol just gave them a head start to get in touch with you again.

4. Rousing Your Jealousy So You Would Notice Them

Have they suddenly started posting a lot about their new life on social media? Chances are they're most certainly trying hard to make you sit up and take notice of them. If they're hanging out with a lot of people that you've never seen or heard of and having a fantastic time, then they're trying to make you jealous.

5. They Throw Shade At You

If they're making snide comments or remarks about you or a new partner, they're still clearly hurt and miss you. They might pass a statement on your outfit or your appearance and lash out at you, trying to make you feel as bad as they do. They may also show disapproval of your new date and point out negative things about them. It's clear that they still haven't moved on and clung to that thin thread of hope.

6. They Do Things To Get Your Attention

Do they post stuff that points towards you? Or do they write cute love letters or poems mentioning you? This is a pretty obvious sign that they miss you and want to get back in their life. They might also ask your friends about you and crash those uninvited parties because they want to see you. You might also see them around more than usual.

7. They Hoard Your Stuff

Are they still keeping your shirt/hoodie and making excuses not to give it even when you have asked them a million times? Or are they keeping even the most useless thing that you might have given them years ago? It's probably because they go through this stuff and relive all the old memories associated with them. They're still not ready to give them up and move on.

8. From The Horse's Mouth

The most obvious and straightforward sign that someone misses you. They tell you themself! Some people don't like to play games and do unnecessary things to gain your attention or throw hints and clues at you and wait for you to notice them. They tell you straight away that they miss you and they want to do something about it.

Conclusion

Now that you have all the signs on your plate, it's up to you whether you want to give them a second chance or move on from all of this. The choice is yours!

Chapter 12:

7 Signs You Have Found A Keeper

Are you looking for Mr. or Mrs. Right? Or do you think you have found the right person, but how can you be sure? Sometimes, we meet someone who seems like the person you would want to spend your whole life with, but during those times, someone is in for a quick hook-up. The only partners worth keeping are the ones that give you the positive vibes that you need after a dull and tedious day, the ones that make you feel happy, and your relationship doesn't feel boring at all. Here are signs that you have found a keeper.

1. They Inspire You To Become A Better Person

When we meet someone very kind, helpful and overall a friendly person that person usually inspires us to be better and luckily the world is full of friendly people. Is your partner like this too? Is he warm, kind, and helpful? Does he inspire you to become a better version of yourself? Then you know you have found yourself a keeper. You know you have found the right person when your partner works hard, gives you and his family time, and has his life organized.

2. They Are Always There

There are times when we all suffer when things get tough to handle. At times like these, a person always needs support and love to get through the hard times. If your partner is there for you even when you can't defend yourself and they cheer you up, you know that this is a keeper. A perfect partner is someone who knows how to make you laugh even when you are crying, your partner will never believe the things people talk about behind your back, and he would never hesitate to lend you a hand when you need some help.

3. They Know You More Than Yourself

Sometimes it fascinates us how someone can know us more than we know ourselves; it feels perfect when someone knows how or what we are thinking. If your partner knows what you are feeling without telling them, then they are the one. Does your partner know what you are comfortable with? Can they tell when you feel upset? Do they motivate you to do better and ask you to chase after your dreams? If so, then don't waste more time thinking if this is the right person for you because it is.

4. Your Interests Are Common

Sure, opposites attract, but too many differences are not usually suitable for someone's relationship. It would help if you had a common interest with your partner, like having common beliefs, values, and religious perspectives. When you agree on these things, your bond will become more robust, and you would find it very easy to live with that person.

5. They Are Honest With You

Finding an honest person is a tiring thing to do; many people lie more than twice a day, but how can that affect your relationship? The right one may lie about small things that don't matter that much, like whether the color suits you or not; they may say those things to make you feel good about yourself, but lying about other things like financial status, health, or fidelity can be more serious. A true keeper would never keep these things from you, and they would always be honest with you even if the truth upsets you.

6. They Don't Feel Tired Of You

Although everyone needs some space, even from the person they love the most, he will never get tired of you if he is the one. Your partner will never feel bored with you; on the contrary, your partner will never get tired of looking at you, admiring you, being with you, and above all, love you. When a person is so in love with you that they want to spend every second of their life with you, then you know you have found a keeper.

7. You Are A Part Of Their Dreams

Can your partner not even imagine your life without you? Has your partner already planned his future, and you are a big part of it? If so, you know that this one's a keeper. You both have reached a point in your lives where even thinking about living without each other sounds absurd, and then you know that you have found a keeper.

Conclusion

A keeper is someone that loves, cherishes, and cares for you like no one has ever had. Don't worry if you haven't found your keeper, and it is just a matter of time before you do because, for every one of us, there is someone out there.

Chapter 13:

6 Gestures That Make People Feel Loved

"Actions speak louder than words ', this phrase is commonly used around us, but hardly anyone knows the real meaning of this phrase. This phrase tells us something about love and the importance of a person. Our actions define us. These actions affect the people around us, it speaks to them in words, we can't speak in. Loving someone is not just enough. You need to show your love, and sometimes the smallest of gestures can make you feel more loved than ever. Everyone wants to feel loved and cared about, and if you truly love them, then show your love, even if it is through a straightforward small text saying, "I miss you." Here are a few ways to make people feel loved.

1. Write Them Notes

Waking up to a heartwarming note on your bedside tables makes someone's day. So whenever you want to show someone how much you love them, just leave them a letter or card. It doesn't matter if you write a few words, either thanking them or telling them how strong they are. These actions affect people the most. It makes them feel loved and, beyond all, appreciated. It also shows that you care about making them feel happy. This note or card will bring a bright smile to their lovely faces.

2. Take Their Favourite Food

"The way to a person's heart is through the stomach," a saying that is quite famous in some parts of the world. Who doesn't feel happy when they get to eat their favorite food? So, whoever this person is that you want to make feel loved, on your way back from work, stop by at their favorite restaurant, buy their favorite dish and surprise them with it. Firstly, they will feel loved knowing that you remembered their favorite word and secondly, the food, of course. Now you know whenever someone's feeling low, bring them their favorite food, it'll take their minds off the stressful thing, and they would feel thankful for you.

3. Remind Them Of Their Importance

As easy as it sounds, expressing love is a tricky thing to do. There have been times when we all love someone but don't express it because we feel shy and as a result, they don't feel loved. As everyone grows up, it is easy to feel alone in this world, so always remind people around you how important they are. Tell people you love them, I love you is just a three-word sentence, but the meaning it holds is more profound than the ocean, so don't hesitate and make your loved ones feel loved.

4. Surprise Them

Everyone has different hobbies, and some people like makeup. Someone prefers football over everything else. As everyone is interested in other things, we often hear them talk about these things. Sometimes they talk about how they want something, but they are either saving up for it or don't have the time. Surprise them with things they have talked about and feel excited about. This makes that person feel loved and cared about. They know that you listen to them, and this quality is something that not everyone has.

5. Listen To Them

As I said before, listening is a quality that people often look at in others. We all need that one person who will listen to us and won't interrupt us when we tell them about our day. People feel grateful when they remember that there is still someone that will listen to them no matter what.

6. Include Them In Things That Matter To You

We talked about their interests but remembered you are important too, don't forget about yourself in the process and don't we all know the person who cares about us will always want to know about our lives and support your decisions. So please include them in things that are important to you, fill them in on the ongoing drama of your life, and inform them about your decisions before you take a step ahead.

Conclusion

When you make someone feel loved, you feel happy, and so do they. Isn't it amazing how easily, by following these steps, you can make someone feel loved? So don't hesitate. Go ahead and show them your love because life's too short to stay hesitant.

Chapter 14:

7 Relationship Goals For Your First Year of Marriage

<u>Newlywed life</u> can be a bit of a topsy-turvy world: You're thankful to be done with all of <u>the wedding planning</u>, yet you miss it-at least a little bit. Where once you were only looking toward the future, you now find yourself gazing at the rear view, thinking about how it all went by so fast. Rest assured, this is actually <u>only the first chapter</u> of everything that's to come in your life together, which means that there's no time like the present to set your sights on these <u>year one marriage goals</u>.

1. Make A Plan For Printing Your Wedding Photos

Finally getting to see to your professional wedding photos is such a happy moment in those first few weeks of married life. On the other hand, realizing how much they're going to cost to have printed and framed can leave you feeling the sticker shock. Don't be deterred; these are keepsakes that will last a lifetime. And don't forget you've got wedding cash!

2. Order An Official Copy Of Your Marriage Certificate

How your signed marriage license is officially filed with the county clerk's office depends on the protocol of your wedding venue or planner. Just make sure that you paid the extra fee to have a copy sent to your home address, too. It's an official document that you won't need often, but when you do need it you'll definitely want to have it.

3. Break Out The Good Stuff

Crystal, silver, porcelain, China-make a point in year one to start using some of the truly special entertaining pieces you received as wedding gifts, and not just during the holidays. They'll add a touch of elegance to any dinner party and will be a focal point of many memorable evenings to come.

4. Print Out Your Vows

Whether you used the traditional vows or wrote your own, keeping a copy of the words that you can refer back to throughout the year can keep your relationship on solid footing. "Your wedding vows are an antidote to your worst instincts,". "They really force us to rethink what's important and what we value. By and large, wedding vows come from our best and our higher self." Think of them as your own personal GPS-a map toward the person you wish you were. "The wedding vows tell us how to aspire to be, and how to treat our partner when our partner is less than their stellar self. If one person can hold steady and remember their vows when a fight starts, it can help settle the other person down."

5. Compliment Each Other Every Day

Every engaged couple hears warnings about not taking each other for granted, but that's a vague goal. Pearson suggests quantifying it with a specific plan during your first year of marriage: "Once a day, tell your partner what you love, value, appreciate, and respect about them." Whether you send a text thanking him for making coffee in the morning or bring her that just-published novel she has on her wish list, small acts can make a big impact. "These gestures done every day start to build in a foundation of connection. "It forces you to think consciously about your partner instead of getting into that habit of letting things slide."

6. Argue (When You Need To)

One of my favourite metaphors for a healthy marriage comes from the history of the British Navy. "They ruled the world because of their navy, but they were willing to do something others didn't,": Periodically pull the boats out of the water and remove barnacles and seaweed from the wooden hulls-before those growths weakened the integrity of the structure or slowed the ship's ability to manoeuvre. "Guess what the parallels are in marriage?" "Resentment, passivity, letting things build up without talking about them, being afraid to create a fight by bringing something up-and then gradually you start to disappear from the marriage. You have to do the work to keep the barnacles scraped off."

7. Plan For Year Two

On <u>your first anniversary</u>, we suggest getting your wedding vows out again (you can use that copy you've been referencing during your fights), and taking stock of how you kept them. "This is an exercise in self-evaluation about being dedicated to coming from your higher self," "Do not evaluate, criticize, judge, or say anything negative about your partner's list, or tell them how they can improve." Instead, consider the promises you made and how you followed through, and imagine the adjustments you could make that would turn you into a better partner for your spouse in the year (and years) to come.

Chapter 15:

10 Signs You've Outgrown Your Friendship

There is almost no one in this world that doesn't have a friend. Some of us even have ten best friends. It all depends on two factors. First is that you have to pick a type of friend and second one is that you find them in this life. Mostly everyone has. Since childhood, you might have had lots of friends. But, did they stay? We eventually have to leave them behind even if we don't want to. It's important to know when to leave them behind, and here are ten signs that you've outgrown your friendship.

1. You Disregard Them

When you've outgrown your friendship with someone, you ignore them. You forget spending time with them. It is unhealthy for a company to disregard each other in any way. So, you naturally drive apart from them. You start to choose different places to hang instead of hanging around with them like you used to.

2. You Pretend

When you are with a friend, all you want is to be yourself. And when you feel like you need to pretend like someone else or like your old self, that's a red flag. You might not fall into each other's expectations of grownups. And it disappoints you both. Compatibility is a key to friendship.

3. Lack Of Effort

Friendship has to grow in the right places, and if it doesn't, then it's not meant to work out. When there are no efforts from even one side, then you both will break apart. One-sided friendship is draining and tiring. We might be ghosting them without even noticing, so it is always better to cut them off.

4. You Get Awkward Around Each Other

One thing that is the most wondrous about friendship is that you can be comfortable around each other even in silence. If you are finding that peaceful silence awkward, then it's an outgrown friendship. It will only make this friendship a burden to you and them. Getting out of this tricky situation means getting out of your company with them.

5. You have nothing to discuss:

Communication is what makes a friendship stronger. When you got nothing to talk about, then you don't have to talk to them at all. There is always something to talk about, and it only depends on the person we are willing to tell. You need to find a person that you want to listen to you.

6. You Both Are Going Different Ways

Life takes everyone on a different path. When you and your friend choose other ways, then it's natural for you to weaken your bond with each other. You both will make new friends according to your phases in life, and that is not such a bad deal. Letting go would be healthy in this situation and for your good.

7. Support Is Unequal

Supporting each other is extremely important in friendship. And if you or your friend doesn't have this quality, you are not a good match. Sometimes, in times of need. That's all that one wants. Advice in this situation may seem like disagreeing.

8. You Keep Secrets

Sharing your day, feelings, and thoughts with your friends sounds like a regular activity for all of us. But some might not agree. When you start to keep things from each other, then that is your weak spot. That is the time you should realize that they are just there for a tag of friend and not playing the actual part.

9. You Don't Understand Each Other Anymore

One of the things that keeps a friendship strong is the compatible understanding between the two of you. And if one of you fails to understand the other one, then you've outgrown your company. It's the aspect that completes you both, and without it, you both are just on loose ends.

10. You Don't Have Any More Familiar Grounds

It was the mutual interest in certain things that bought you two close enough to be friends. Eventually, you both will find different things likable. Your friend might hate those things and never tell you. But when you sit together and find nothing to talk about. That is where you have to end this friendship.

Conclusion:

Friends might have a significant impact on our lives, but we have to let them go eventually. You will make lots of friends along the way. Leaving one behind doesn't make you the wrong person. It makes you strong one.

Chapter 16:

10 Signs To Leave A Relationship

According to a tinder survey, around 40% of millennials won't stay with the wrong person just for the sake of keeping their long-term relationship. Sometimes it's better to let go of the person you've been dating for a long time if you notice that your relationship doesn't make you happy or, even worse, makes you feel uncomfortable and depressed.

A study suggests that certain signs can tell you it's time to leave your partner. And while they don't always mean all is lost and there's no point in fighting for your love, they could help you figure out if there's a problem.

1. You Keep Breaking Up And Getting Back Together

According to research, on average, more than 1/4 of couples will break up and get back together at some point.And this might even end up becoming a never-ending cycle of on-again-off-again relationships. Maybe you're second-guessing yourself and decide to give your partner a second chance, or you're afraid to let go and move on. But it's important to break that cycle because this kind of relationship might not do you or your partner any good.

2. You Don't Like Yourself

Not liking yourself in a relationship can be exhausting, especially if you don't like who you've become because of your partner. Maybe you've distanced yourself from your family that you love or feel less motivated to try to achieve your goals because of them. If your partner is constantly bringing you down in any way, instead of inspiring and being supportive, it's time to cut them out of your life.

3. Your Partner Is Constantly Criticizing You

It's one thing to mention what you don't like about how your partner behaves, which can be a healthy thing to do and help you better communicate with each other and improve yourself. But it's a different thing when your partner criticizes your personality and character.

4. You're Afraid Of Being Alone

Fear of being single is not a good enough reason to stay in a relationship, especially if there're signs that your partner isn't right for you and you're not happy. Studies have shown that people who are afraid of being single settle for any partner just for the sake of being in a relationship, no matter how this affects its quality. However, that doesn't make the situation any better, and that fear will also make it harder to get out of an unsatisfying relationship.

5. You Live In The Past

If you think about how much fun you used to have with your partner and how happy you were with them in the <u>past</u> more than you enjoy the actual relationship in the present, this is a red flag. Being more in love with the memory of who your partner was or what your relationship used to be like won't bring you happiness once you realize that this is the only thing keeping you from leaving. So it's important to distinguish between what's gone and not coming back and what's real and worth staying for.

6. Your Partner Is Too Unpredictable And Intense

Some people can be nice and charming one moment and then suddenly angry the next. This behavior can make you feel scared and intimidated, and you always need to walk on eggshells around them to prevent triggering them, even in little ways. That means your partner is emotionally <u>volatile</u>.

7. Your Relationship Is Superficial

When you've just met someone, it's understandable that you won't immediately open up to them and reveal your deepest secrets. Your conversations will be focused on more simple things, like your hobbies or your job. But with time, it's natural for you and your partner to grow close, which means you aren't afraid to show your more vulnerable side and discuss more serious topics.

8. Your Relationship Is One-Sided

If your partner only wants to be with you when they need you, for example, when they had a bad day at work or some other problems, this is not a good sign. They might be using you to get attention while not caring about what you need. And if you constantly do all the work in your relationship, supporting your partner when they don't do the same for you, you might be stuck in a <u>toxic</u> relationship.

9. Your Partner Often Says He'll Leave You

If your partner threatens to leave you, for example during fights, or when they can't make you do what they want, this might be a form of psychological <u>manipulation</u>. They're using your fear of abandonment to control you. This controlling behavior might extend to different areas of your life, so it's important to recognize it and put a stop to it before you get hurt.

10. You Don't Want To Share Good News With Your Partner

If something <u>positive</u> has happened in your life, but it doesn't even cross your mind anymore to share it with your partner, it might be a sign that your relationship is in trouble. This might mean that you feel like your happiness is irrelevant to your partner because they don't care about you as much as they used to. And if that's true, and they don't genuinely encourage you and feel happy when you succeed, it might be time to leave.

Do you recognize these signs from your previous relationships? How did you decide that it was time to break up?

Chapter 17:

10 Life Skills You Need To Have

What is life?

Nobody has ever fully exhausted the explanation of what life entails. It is a mystery that hitherto has never been completely unraveled. It is an examination where every candidate has a different question paper and the marking scheme is adhered to ruthlessly.

We can learn from the experience of our predecessors how they managed to meander through the obstacles of life. They must have a few life hack tricks that are indispensable in making our life easier. Here are ten necessary life skills to ace the game of life:

1. Assertiveness

It is the skill of being honest and transparent with yourself and the people you interact with. The quality of honesty is rare making it thoroughly sought for. Nobody wants to deal with dishonest people because they can sink their boat of success.

Assertiveness or lack of it distinguishes nobles from commoners. It works magic to those who practice it. People consider them reliable and the future calls out to them to secure it.

2. Integrity

Integrity is a wider scope of assertiveness. Apart from being honest, people of integrity uphold a higher standard of morality. They have hard stances against vices of every nature and cannot compromise on anything that hurts their belief.

As a life skill, integrity secures you the moral authority to condemn societal ills. It becomes even more important to build a reputation of integrity if you are a public figure. Furthermore, integrity protects its holders from the effects of vices like corruption.

3. Critical Thinkers

Critical thinking involves deeper reasoning of the motives behind actions, the consequences of choices, and the impact of alternative decisions we could make.

It is important to develop critical thinking to evaluate matters before arriving at conclusions. There is little to no chance of having regrets if you have critical thinking.

4. Self-Love

Self-love is caring for yourself as you do others. It does not lean to selfishness but according to yourself an equal treatment as the people you interact with.

Do not overlook self-love because it is a skill that few people have mastered. Those who lack it suffer from a bruised ego and low self-esteem.

5. Interpersonal Skills

They are skills that enable one to interact properly with people they meet. Personal relationships have reduced drastically due to advancements in technology. People prefer virtual meetings to physical ones.

You need to stand out by being unique and embrace interpersonal skills. You will be able to make friendships faster and build a network of trustworthy friends.

6. Self-Confidence

How can other people have confidence in you if you doubt yourself? Self-confidence is key in winning the trust of other people. You need to exude confidence in the values you believe for other people to follow suit.

In a business world, believe in yourself and the products or services you offer for clients to value your input. Self-confidence is not pride but a demonstration of competence.

7. Creativity

It is the ability to think outside the ordinary and come up with original suggestions and ideas. Creativity is limitless and does not discriminate against age or gender. Everyone is creative at their level. It is their complexity to wind simple ideas into great sustainable ventures that increase the value of creative people.

Creativity augments the value a person brings to the table. It is a necessary life skill that raises the quality of life from a personal level.

8. Arbitration Skills

Arbitration is the act of being an impartial judge in a conflict between two or more parties. Since conflicts are inevitable, it comes in handy to unite the warring groups. How would life be without people to justly arbitrate conflicts?

It is an important life skill because it makes one a peacemaker. Moreover, arbiters largely live peaceful lives because they have learned from the mistakes of those they help.

9. Analytical Skills

A critical analysis of situations is necessary to make informed decisions. Analytical skills enable one to distinguish right from wrong. They can decipher deception from afar even when it is properly concealed.

There comes a time when we are left alone without guidance and find our way around unfamiliar territories. We require strong analytical skills to remain afloat.

10. Fast Thinking

There is often a lot of emphasis on correct thinking and logic and we forget how fast we need to do it. It is not enough that we can arrive at correct conclusions. It is useless if we cannot do it faster to save an already worse situation.

Fast thinking is a skill only taught in the school of life and not classrooms. Learn to develop fast solutions to problems because time makes all the difference.

In conclusion, these ten life skills are just a few from a pool of many that are essential for survival. They make life easier for all those who have them.

Chapter 18:

6 Ways to Create A Great Online Dating Profile

Venturing out into the online dating scene is not easy, especially when it comes to creating a dating profile that lets others know who you are. Consequently, it's common to feel pressure to either write a lot or to be the funniest or most interesting person on the app. But the truth is that no one expects you to be perfect. Sometimes it's the simplest and most honest dating profiles that are the most effective.

Remember that an online dating profile is basically personal marketing. As a result, you'll want to do everything you can to put your best foot forward. Knowing how to capture your own personality, idiosyncrasies, interests, and general outlook on life in just a few short paragraphs can be daunting even for the best writers. So, here are a few tips on how to make your online dating profile stand out in the crowd.

1. Choose Your Photos Wisely

Photos are one of the best ways to introduce yourself to strangers. But, too many times, online dating hopefuls will select a profile picture that isn't completely clear or hides their face in some way. People want to see you and get a sense of who you are. So, select a photo that shows your full face, hopefully with a smile. Additionally, if you have the option to upload multiple photos, do it. After all, it takes more than one photo to reveal more about your personality to others.

2. Fill in All the Fields

One mistake a lot of people make is not taking advantage of the tools the app provides. For instance, if the dating site you're on allows you to have seven photos, then provide seven photos. If the app provides the option to verify your photos, then take advantage of it.

The key is that you make use of every tool they provide. The more effort you put into your online dating profile to show others you're available and interested, the more responses you will likely receive.

3. Provide Plenty of Examples

Try to make your profile interesting by giving examples when talking about things you enjoy. For instance, instead of saying that you enjoy reading, tell readers your favorite book. Or, if you like hiking, tell them your favorite trail.

The more you go into detail, the more likely a person might get excited and think "they're perfect for me." On the other hand, if your profile is surface-level and generic, it's easy to get lost in the pile and be dismissed. You can even provide details of the type of person you are looking for or the types of dating experiences you might enjoy.

4. Be Concise

Even though details are important, it's still smart to be somewhat selective about the information you choose to share. When it comes to writing a dating profile, a short paragraph or two is enough. You should give an overview of who you are, but not tell your entire life story all at once. Remember, you want to give people a reason to message you and get to know you, and there's something fun about maintaining a little bit of mystery!

5. Create Opportunities to Connect

One of the best things you can do with your dating profile is to provide ways for people to start a conversation with you. For instance, once you are matched with someone, they are going to view your profile and, if you're interested, try to think of something to say when they reach out. Consequently, you want to be sure your profile provides enough information that they could ask you a question about something in it.

Or, if you want, include a conversation starter. Apps such as <u>Hinge</u> provide prompts for you to fill out with details of yourself, many with the implication of starting a conversation. "Change my mind about...", "Two truths and a lie", and "What I want to know about you" are all fun ways for you to put some information out there that makes it easy for people to reach out and break the ice.

6. Be Honest

When it comes to online dating, it can be tempting to stretch the truth a bit in order to present yourself in the best possible light. But, the majority of people prefer honesty over perfection. So, make a concerted effort to be as open and honest as you can. After all, you are just setting yourself up for unneeded stress and disappointment if you try to come off as someone you're not.

At first, it can seem overwhelming to create an online dating profile. But the truth is, you just need to follow a few simple rules: Be honest, be yourself, and be specific. If you follow those guidelines and couple the information with some solid photographs, you will be fielding matches in no time.

Chapter 19:

How To Stop Getting In Your Own Way

Are there valid reasons why you can't get things done? Absolutely. In fact, many times, external forces are working against you — think a sick child, flat tire, or global pandemic. There are, however, times when it turns out that we're our own biggest obstacle. We also call this self-sabotage. And, it can be brutal when it comes to productivity and our wellbeing. The good news? You can conquer this by getting out of your way. And, it's feasible by trying out the following techniques.

Remember Your Why

Instead of going through the motions and doing things for no reason, reconnect with your purpose. If you can't connect the dots between the activity and the big picture, then stop doing it. That doesn't mean avoiding tasks that you don't always enjoy. For example, as a new business owner, you might dread bookkeeping. However, it's an essential responsibility if you want your business to thrive. Remind yourself that maintaining your finances, sticking to a budget, and preparing your taxes can help you reach your business goals. And, as your business scales up, you can eventually hand this off to someone else.

Acknowledge Your Strengths

A strength is an activity that strengthens you. It doesn't have to be something that you excel at. Instead, it's something that you look forward to and "leaves you feeling energized. A strength is more appetite than ability, and it's that appetite that drives us to want to do it again; practice more; refine it to perfection. The appetite leads to the practice, which leads to performance. Leveraging your strengths and managing around your weaknesses isn't just about making yourself feel better. It's about conditioning yourself to contribute the best of yourself every day. It's about performance.

Nothing Compares To You — Except You

You bust your tail but aren't as productive as a colleague. You see that a friend just bought a new car or are enjoying a luxurious vacation. And, that just leaves you feeling like a failure. But, as Mark Twain once said, "comparison is the death of joy." Research backs that statement up. Comparing yourself to others leads to low self-confidence and depression. It can also make you green with envy, deplete motivation, and doesn't bring you closer to your goals. In short, if you measure yourself against others, you're always going to come short. Instead, practice gratitude. And, better yet, compare yourself by tracking your progress and celebrating what you've accomplished.

Run With The Right Crowd

Are you familiar with saying, "you are what you eat?" "Well, it's also true when it comes to who you keep company with. You may not realize this. But, the people you interact with on a daily basis directly influence who you are and what you do. Make sure you surround yourself with people who encourage you and hold you accountable—people from who you can learn positive habits from.

Remove Unnecessary Pressure

Life is hectic enough. So, why make things worse by overcommitting or setting unrealistic expectations? Be realistic about what you can actually accomplish. If you don't have the availability or skillset, just say "no." For example, if you're calendar is already packed, decline time requests like unnecessary meetings or talking to a friend on the phone for two hours.

Engage In Self-Care

Some might consider self-care as a selfish act. In reality, it's making time for activities that leave you feeling calm and energized. These are vital in supporting your mental, physical, and emotional wellbeing. Examples can include going for a walk, journaling, hobbies, meditating, or taking a shower. Since time might appear to be a concern, add self-care to your calendar. For instance, you could leave an hour blank from 1 pm to 2 pm to spend however you like.

Avoid Ruminating

Ruminating is a cycle of repeating thoughts that you just can't shake. As a result, this can impair thinking and problem-solving. And, it can cause you to get stuck in your own head. To break free of these swirling thoughts, distract yourself. Examples are doing chores, reading, or calling a friend. You can also question your beliefs, set more attainable goals, and take small action steps to solve problems.

.

Chapter 20:

10 Tips To Stop Liking Your Crush

Very often, people experiencing a major crush know their expectations are unrealistic. They may even be aware that they don't have a chance with this crush. Maybe it's incompatibility. Or maybe the other person is taken. One thing's for sure: it can feel heart breaking and all-consuming. If you want to know how to get rid of a crush and stop obsessing, it's important to consider the situation in objective terms. So, what do you do if you find yourself caught up in a crush? Below are some ideas on how to get rid of a crush:

1. Talk To Them

Find out if you have anything in common. Ask what's going on in their lives. As mentioned above, you might be surprised to find that their personality is nothing like you'd imagined it to be. You may even find that you disagree on important topics, or that they're intellectually lacking which can lead you to being over your crush.

2. Do Not Avoid Your Crush

In doing so, you may keep the fantasy alive. You owe it to yourself to have a real conversation with them. You may find there is no chemistry between the two of you and decide to move on.

3. Get Busy With Other Aspects Of Life

You had a life before meeting this person, and that life continues despite your feelings for him or her. Get back to that life, and focus on the things that bring you joy. Distractions that you find fulfilling can take your mind off of your crush and remind you that you have a lot going for you with or without this person in your life. Focus on your education, your work, volunteering for a charity, or even learning a new hobby. Don't over exert yourself while trying to get to know your crush.

4. Spend Time With Family And Friends

surrounding yourself with the people that mean the most to you-people who love and respect you for you--can remind you that you are whole, with or without a partner.

5. Confide In Your Loved Ones About Your Crush

They may surprise you with a great piece of advice. For instance, a parent or aunt might share why they think you have a crush on this person and what that says about you. Or perhaps they have had their own experience with a crush and can impart some words of wisdom about how to handle the situation. Perhaps you have dating patterns that you don't see, and they can shed some light on your choices. Maybe this new perspective on your love life could help you figure out how to move on.

6. Question Yourself About The Origin Of This Crush

Take the emphasis off of him or her, and focus on yourself. Why do you feel this way? Could there have been other circumstances that led to the crush? Maybe you were feeling down the day you first met, and your crush smiled at you at the right moment? Sometimes, feelings can be situational, and when that person becomes an actual part of our lives, we may feel differently.

7. Take A Look At The Reality Of The Situation In Its Entirety

is this a fantasy relationship that you've created in your mind? Ask yourself, "does this person have the qualities of the person i want to be with? Or am i projecting them onto him or her?

8. Give Yourself A Chance To Grieve

If you do believe, after trying all of the above, that you've missed out on your true love, give yourself space to feel sad about it. Acknowledge and sit with those feelings; don't ignore them or bury them because this will only lead to unresolved feelings that you'll have to address down the road. Or if you've determined that your crush was just that--a crush--allow yourself to grieve the feelings that were there. You probably spent a good amount of time fantasizing, and that can be fun and exciting. When the fantasy ends, it can be jarring and uncomfortable.

9. Stop Following Them On Social Media

You do not need reminders of him or her or updates about what he or she is doing every minute of the day. Furthermore, most people only post the best of what's happening in their lives, so you will likely not be looking at the full picture.

10. Lastly, The Most Fun Option

Put yourself out there to remind yourself that there are plenty of other people who want to date you. You can join an online dating site, ask your friends to set you up, or join a club that explores one of your interests. All of these are great ways to meet new and interesting people.

Chapter 21:

6 Signs You May Be Lonely

What is that one emotion that leads us to anxiety, depression, or stress? People often feel this emotion when they have no one around to support them. That is being lonely. What is being lonely? "When one is unable to find life's meaning," or simply put, it is the feeling of isolation. You often find yourself in a corner then outside with friends or family. Sometimes, these emotions are triggered by discouragement by close ones and negativity of life. We try to bear it alone rather than risking the judgment of others. We try to hide it as much as possible. Then, eventually, it becomes a habit. Then even if it's news worth sharing, we keep it to ourselves.

Loneliness can drive a person to harm themselves, either physically or mentally, or both too. It can change our lives drastically. Going out seems to be a burden. It feels tiresome even to move an inch. So, we tend to stay in one place, probably alone. But it doesn't always mean that you are feeling sad. Sometimes you feel happy being alone. It all depends on how you look at things.

1. Feeling Insecure

When we look around us, we see people every day. This type of connection with people can lead to two conclusions. Positive or negative. A positive attitude may lead to appreciation. However, negative emotions will lead to insecurities. This insecurity will lead us to go out as little as possible. And whatever we hate about us, we feel it more prominent. Eventually, we never go out at all. Because of the fear that people might judge us at our worst trait. We think that even our family is against us, which makes it even more difficult.

2. Anger Becomes A Comrade

It becomes hard to express what we feel to others. When we feel like there is no one we can genuinely tell our feeling to, they bottle up. We start to bottle up our emotions to don't get a chance to tell others about them. And those bottle-up emotions turn into anger the most easily. Even the slightest thing could make us aggressive. We get angry over all petty stuff, and gradually, it becomes our release to all the emotion. It becomes easier to show your anger than other emotions.

3. It Starts To Hurt Us Physically

Stress is one of the feelings you get out of being lonely. It is only natural that you stress about everything when you are alone in a situation.

Scientifically, it is proven that staying alone most of the time raises our stress hormone, and it becomes a heart problem in the future. Most of us have experienced the tightening of our chest at times. That is when our stress hormone raises it builds up around our heart. It may also result in inflammation and some vascular problems. So, being lonely all the time may be physically harmful to us, and we should take it seriously.

4. Highly Harmful To Mental Health

Mental health is just as important as physical health. We need to focus on both equally. Loneliness can be harmful to our mental health in many ways. It often leads to hallucinations. It causes depression and anxiety. These types of mental occurrences are proven fatal if not dealt with immediately. It also drives us to overthink, which is equally as harmful as others. Isolation keeps your brain in a constant phase of resentment.

5. Lack Of Hope and Self-Compassion

Getting lonely sometimes is okay. It gets serious when you do not want to let go of it. When there is no hope, it feels like there is no reason to return—staying alone forces you into feeling empty and unwanted, thus, losing hope of ever being wanted again. Because discouragement surrounds us, we feel safe staying alone most of the time. We lose all the passion we once had, and it makes us dull. Things that once we loved doing feel like a burden. Gradually, we become addicted.

6. Negativity

Positivity and negativity are two aspects of daily life. And in life, when loneliness is our companion, we choose negativity to go through our day. Everything seems to be too much work, and everything in life seems dark. Negativity is the only thing we keep because it looks more suitable to lonely people. It causes emotional harm to people and tends to get in the way of an average daily routine. However, the negative side is what we choose every day.

Conclusion

We can feel lonely even after being surrounded by people because it's just something people feel in themselves. They don't realize that there are people who are willing to talk to them. Being lonely can cause one a lot of harm and disrupt all the day's work. But it doesn't always mean that lonely people are unhappy. Loneliness can bring peace too.

Chapter 22:

6 Ways To Transform Your Thinking

Changing your mindset isn't easy, but an open and positive attitude. Personal growth contributes to our choices to achieve physical, emotional, and spiritual well-being. Even something as simple as changing your mind can change your life. It's essential to take time for your mindset. During this period, we begin to understand ourselves, making us more compassionate and patient with ourselves. Our societies and cultures thrive in the professions that life brings to our lives and our tables. In this regard, the use of "bandage" solutions and rapid remedies to overcome certain obstacles in our lives have implications. These decisions never last long and are a matter of time and effort to slow down, ground up, and shift focus. Changing your mind means becoming more optimistic and giving your mind the breathing space it needs to grow and expand. It's about looking at everything that doesn't work for you and being open to other methods that might help.

1. Practice Mindfulness

To adopt a more positive mindset, you must first recognize your current mindset. As you develop mindfulness, you can recognize and identify habituated thought patterns and then decide whether to use them or not. Mindfulness creates a distance between you and your thoughts, allowing you to see yourself separate from them. Incorporate mindfulness into your morning or evening routine and sit quietly for a few minutes (and practice gradually increasing the amount of time). When a thought comes to mind, turn your attention to your breathing instead of clinging to it.

2. Address Your Inner Critic

Your inner critic likes to convince you that it's not true, which often makes you feel pretty bad. Think of this voice as separate from you. Challenge the lie he is trying to feed you. Ask yourself. Is it true? Is there any evidence to support this claim? Another way is to thank this inner voice for their opinion and then say "no." I prefer not to fall into these negative thoughts. Alternatively, you may choose shorter, more direct answers, such as Not Now or Delete.

3. Know Your Triggers

It is essential to be aware of certain people, situations, and situations to trigger more negative thoughts. Meeting your boss or making important life decisions can make you overly critical of yourself or question your worth. Once you become aware of your triggers, you can better prepare to control your thoughts than go back to your old negative thinking patterns. It is also helpful to see which cognitive biases, such as those mentioned above, recur most often.

4. Write It Out

Writing down your feelings on paper is a great way to relieve your thoughts and learn more about them. We often don't realize how harmful our thoughts are. Negative thinking patterns become habitual over time and usually go unnoticed. Taking notes makes it easier to identify areas that need attention. You can also ask questions as soon as they appear in the article to ensure they are accurate and relevant. If not, let them go or replace them with more positive thoughts. Writing in a diary, the first thing you do when you wake up in the morning is the perfect time to write down your stream of consciousness on paper.

5. Recite A Mantra

Shouting out a mantra or positive affirmation is a great way to break free from your current negative thoughts. When you feel that something negative is coming, you can make it a habit to recite or focus on it several times throughout the day. You can choose words or phrases that remind you to focus on the present and focus more on the positive.

6. Change Your Surroundings

Sometimes the thoughts are so loud that it is best to change the physical environment. Go for a walk, run or meet friends in nature. The point is to engage in something other than a negative cycle so you can get back to the problem when you're in a cleaner space. Choose your favourite activity or place, and you will feel better. If you need to be with others, have people around you to encourage you to think positively. (Avoid the trigger!)

Negative stereotypes of thoughts are challenging to break, especially when habituated. Patterns that have existed for years don't disappear overnight, so it's essential to show compassion and patience for yourself as you work.

Chapter 23:

10 Habits of Sergey Brin

When you say "the apple doesn't fall far from the tree," you're undoubtedly referring to Serge Brin's facts. Although he paused his Ph.D. studies to start Google, the man appears to have followed in his parents' footsteps. Sergey comes from a well-educated family; his mother is a NASA researcher, and his father is a math professor.

Sergey Brin is the co-founder of Google and Alphabet Inc., a computer scientist, and a highly successful entrepreneur. The Russian techie met Larry Page while pursuing his Ph.D. studies, and they both dropped out to start Google. Despite being a latecomer to the search game, Google now reigns supreme.

Here are 10 Habits of Sergey Brine.

1. Disable Temptation

Just like Sergey Brin, when handling a matter of great importance, practices self-control and disable any temptations or distractions. Disable your phone when necessary, install apps that help you maintain control to stay focused. Having a habit Stacker is also an excellent tool for helping you build the focus needed.

2. Don't Think About Money

When it comes to success, most people think of money. But when Brin and Larry were creating Google, money was far from their minds. They wanted to create a search engine that people could rely on to get information on anything on the internet. Once you create something of value, be sure to rip greatness in the end as Brin is now.

3. Worry Less About the Roadblocks

Brin once said that the success journey is a journey multiple failures. Many young people are prone to seeing massive mountains, but he sees only a small one to climb. It's all about your perfective to approaching life and focusing on overcoming minor problems. The more you focus on the mountains, the more anxious you become and the less productive you'll be.

4. Shut the Door

Increasing the ability to stay "locked into something" is extremely important to Sergey, which drives Google's development. Close the door, both literally and metaphorically. This entails preventing the outside world from interfering with your project's progress. When you close your door, you are signalling to the world that you are working.

5. Greatness Comes From Unexpected Places

Has anyone ever made fun of you for unexpected reasons? Has anyone ever questioned your abilities because of who they perceived you to be? Say no more – you already know the truth and your capabilities. Sergey and his co-founder made Google from their dorm room, and it took off quickly such that by 2000, it had collected over one billion URLs. You can achieve great things no matter where you come from, where you started, or now.

6. Think Big

Google is one of the world's most excellent, fast, and diverse companies, thanks to Sergey Brin, a daring thinker, and entrepreneur. Google is so flexible and abstract that you wouldn't know its following ideas and inventions. The idea, as Brin insists, is to think big or go home! Without an optimistic attitude or charismatic intuition, your thoughts are not worth a dime.

7. Work With the Appropriate Team

You need a great team working for you, just as Sergey Brin focuses on getting the best talents working for Google for better results. It doesn't matter if you have a small or large company; you can benefit from size. When you go from 1–10 people, you have no idea who they are. At that point, the best course of action would be to continue growing and reaping the benefits of scale.

8. Be an Ambitious Creator

According to the New York Times, Brin may have played a significant role in developing several projects as Google evolved from just a search engine to a large company. He was the key driver behind the most ambitious projects, including Google+, self-driving cars, smart contact lenses, and smart glasses. All you need is an intense desire and determination to put your ideas into action.

9. Be Inquisitive

A curious person like Sergey Brin will always find a thousand reasons to achieve the goals. As he says, "when a dream appears, seize it," it is best to go extra crazy to achieve what you believe in. Just ensure you don't give up on your dreams and strive for the best.

10. Apply Brilliance

Anyone who knows Sergey knows that he truly believes in using his power and knowledge for the greater good. The Economist dubbed him the "Enlightenment Man" for his commitment to using science and logic to solve major global issues. Everyone wants to be successful, but when you see yourself as an innovator, ethical, and trustworthy person, you will be remembered as a game-changer, just as Brin wants to be remembered.

Conclusion

It's pretty clear that Sergey Brin is an intellect personality. His abilities and talents are so unique that it's understandable to envy him or want to be like him. However, once you focus on changing the world, the more likely you'll be recognized among the greatest.

Chapter 24:

6 Signs You Have Found A Real Friend

Life seems easy when we have someone by our side. Everyone makes at least one friend in their life as if it comes naturally. That one person who we can rely on in difficult times. That one person who cares for us when we forget to care for ourselves. Friends are family that we get to choose ourselves. So, we have to decide that person exceptionally carefully. Friends are people who know who you are. You can share both joy and sadness with them without hesitating.

Friends have a significant impact on our lives. They can change us completely and help us shape ourselves into someone better. However, there might be some forgery in your way. Some people consider themselves as your friend, but we fail to notice that it is otherwise. So, it is imperative to choose a friend carefully, while an essential fraction is dependent on our friendship with someone. A good friend is the one whom you can count on to hold you when you require one. A friend is someone who becomes selfless when it comes to us. They always stay by your side as it said, "friends till the end."

1. You Can Be Yourself Around Them

No matter how you behave in front of your family or co-workers, you can always act like yourself in front of your friend. When they give you a sense of comfort, you automatically become yourself. That is the reason you never get tired of a friend. Because who gets tired of being who they are. A friend is a person who accepts us with all our flaws and stays by us even in our worst phase. They find beauty in your imperfections. That type of friend becomes necessary to keep around.

2. A Support For Good And Bad Times

We all are aware that support is what we want in our time of need. To share our difficult times and to share our good news with someone. A friend listens. They listen to whatever you want to ramble to them without complaining. They understand you and try to give to advice as well as possible. They are an excellent shoulder to cry on. They feel joy in your happiness. They feel sadness in your loss. Friends are people who love us, and thus, we give them ours in return.

3. You Trust Each Other

Trust is an essential foundation in any friendship. Otherwise, you are meant to fall apart. It would help if you grew that trust slowly. When you are loyal to each other, then there is nothing that comes between you two. You need to develop that trust slowly. When you are dedicated to each other, then there is nothing that comes between you two. Honesty is a must when it comes to building your trust with each other. If even one of you is lying about anything, then that friendship fails. Even if they didn't keep their promise, you can't trust them.

4. They Hype You Up

They won't fall back on complimenting you when you look your best. But a friend won't hesitate to confront you if you don't look good. That is what we like about them, and they won't make you look bad in front of others. They will make sure you know you are worth it. They will make you work for what you deserve. Friends will always try to hype you up and will accolade you. They know what you like and don't, so they shape you like you want to be shaped.

5. You Share Almost Everything

Two friends are always together in spirits. When something noteworthy happens in your life, you always feel the need to share it with someone. That someone will probably be a friend. You tend to share every little detail of any event of your life with them comfortably. They listen to you. And sometimes, they need to be listened to. That's where you come. You listen to them. Even the most intimate secrets are told sometimes. This exchanging of secrets can only be done when you feel safe sharing them with a person. A friend buries your secrets within themselves.

6. Good Memories

Even the most boring party can take a 360 degree turn when you are with your friend. Times like these call for good memories. It would help if you shared loads of good memories. Even when time passes by, a bad day can make an excellent future memory.

Conclusion

It takes a lot of time, care and love to form a strong bond of friendship. We have to give it our best to keep that bond in good condition. Friends are precious to us, and we should make them feel likewise. And with the right person, friendship can last a lifetime.

Chapter 25:

6 Dating Red Flags To Avoid

When dating someone, there always stands a risk. A risk of not being happy or a threat of choosing the wrong person. That is why elders taught us to make smart decisions smartly. But what can one do when it comes to finding the one. Acknowledging a person you want to date won't be enough. Many factors revolve around dating. That is why it is essential to recognize red flags in your relationship. So, we should never hurry to commit to someone. Take your time. There is a lot more than getting to know this person. When initially dating, we always need to make sure to know where our comfort zone lies.

Red flags are the danger signs of a relationship. It can save you a lot of time and positivity. And it's not necessarily true that only the other person is to blame. Sometimes we fail to give them our part of affection, and gradually it becomes a disaster. Even if we overlook the minor toxicity, ignoring the major red flags is not suitable for you. Don't hesitate to give your opinion.

1. Shortfall Of Trust

The one major thing we all need to date someone is trust. Doubt will only make things difficult for you and your partner. Trusting each other is vital in a relationship. And when you date someone, trust grows slowly. And if your growth is based on lies and cheating, then that trust is as thin as thread. You can't force yourself to trust them either. If it doesn't come naturally, count it as a significant red flag because trust is the first thing that comes when dating someone.

2. Change In Personality

In a relationship, we have often seen people change their personalities around different people. If the same is happening to you, then you have to be careful. If they act differently around you, it indicates that they are not themselves in front of you. That is one major red flag in dating that shouldn't be ignored. They try to act the way you would like, instead of the course you are in. And eventually, they will get frustrated. So, it's better to be yourself around everyone. That way, your relationship will be genuine, and you feel a lot happier.

3. Toxicity

An abusive relationship is the worst kind. When someone is not attentive towards you or shouts at you constantly, you become the submissive one. It would be best if you took a stand for yourself equally. Most of the time, people stay quiet in times like these. But it's to be known that it is a dangerous sign in your dating life. It's a red flag that needs to be taken into notice. You don't have to cope with them; leave them be. Find someone who matches your energy. A toxic person is just as bad as drugs. We need to be careful around them.

4. Feeling Insecure

Sometimes, a relationship that is not meant to be, leaves you feeling insecure about yourself. You constantly question your place in that relationship. Where do you stand in their life? It leaves you thinking about all the flaws you have and examining all the wrong decisions. You have to know that it works both ways. And whoever they are, they have to accept you no matter what. You start to contribute more than your partner when it should be all about equality.

5. Not Being Around Each Other

When we dive into a relationship, we feel the need to be comforted. And when the person opposite you makes you feel uncomfortable, it's a major red flag in your dating life. You both need to make sure to be there for support. If not, then that relationship doesn't hold any significant meaning. If we do not feel secure or satisfied, then what do we get from this relationship? Because that is the most important thing that we might need from someone. But it's essential to play your part as well. Both sides should give their all for their dating to work.

6. Keeps Secret From You

What someone needs in a relationship is to share their lives. Talking is the basis of communication that builds a relationship. But if your partner keeps secrets, then how can you grow together? You always need to speak for better understanding and comfort with each other. If they are acting fishy, you can't spy on them. It's a red flag that you need to catch.

Conclusion

You need someone who provides you with what you deserve. If you feel someone is not suitable for you, then feel free to break up with them. It would help if you were your priority. And make sure others know how important you are to yourself and should be important to them too.

Chapter 26:

6 Ways To Be More Confident In Bed

Confidence is something a lot of people inherit naturally, while others could work on. When you're confident and comfortable in your skin, people assume that you have a reason to be, and then they react and respect you accordingly. You can be confident all you want at work or on dates, but what about being confident in bed? Being confident sexually can be enjoyable for both you and your partner. It isn't just at ease sexual, but also it's comfortable with the way you express and experience your sexuality.

Sexual confidence can be measured by how authentically you can relate intimately either with yourself or your partner and how pure and vulnerable you are in that sexual space where you feel like giving your 100 percent to be yourself and communicate the pleasure you desire. Building your confidence in bed can crucially improve your sex life. Here are some tips on how to be more confident in bed.

1. Do What You're Already Confident In

Even if you are insecure and think you lack sexual skills, there must be at least a tiny thing that you might be good at. Maybe you don't feel confident enough about your kissing skills, but you're a great cuddler, or perhaps you feel shaky about touching and teasing but are good vocally. Focus on what you're good at and polish that skill every time you're in bed with your partner. This will help you boost your confidence and might even convince you to try something new with them.

2. Try Something New

Once you start considering yourself as the master of that one skill you have been practicing, you would end up craving to try new things. Start with the things you're less comfortable with; maybe stepping out of your comfort zone might be enjoyable for you after all. You neither have to perfect the skill nor be a master of it, just trying it out can be fun in itself. It might be helpful to broaden the sexual script so that it doesn't look the same every time and bore your partner, but instead, trying new things can be an excellent adventure for you as well as your partner.

3. Laugh It Off If You Trip Up

You can't be good at everything you try in bed, nor should you be. What matters is how well you keep your attitude, and if you can have fun with it and have a great laugh if things go south, that's an achievement in itself. If you have already built up consistent self-confidence, then you can laugh it out loud on something that you can't get a grip on. After all, there might always be some things you'll be bad at and others in which you'll be a master.

4. Focus On What You Love About Your Body

There are instances where we will be utterly insecure about our bodies and features. There are some physical traits that we don't like but have made peace with, while others that we want but don't appreciate enough. The next time you look in the mirror, focus more on what you like about your face and body, be confident in them, and the things you don't like about yourself will vanish automatically.

5. Wear What Makes You Feel Confident

There is no particular stuff you have to wear or the way you have to look to feel more confident, but if you wear a look that you think looks great, you must go with it. Chances are, you will start feeling better about yourself instantly. If you feel more confident wearing lipstick, then wear it to bed, or if you think sexier wearing a lotion, use it before bed. Do whatever makes you feel like a total hottie.

6. Repeat A Mantra

We have all heard of the phrase "fake it till you make it." So, there's no harm in faking affirmations till you start believing in them. Keep repeating "I'm confident, I've got this" till it gets through. Affirmations increase how positively we feel about ourselves.

Conclusion

The task of becoming confident may seem daunting, but these small sub-tasks are an easy way to start. Another plus point is once you have practiced these techniques in bed, the confidence will spill over into every area of your life.

Chapter 27:

6 Signs You Have A Fear of Intimacy

Intimacy avoidance or avoidance anxiety, also sometimes referred to as the fear of intimacy, is characterized as the fear of sharing a close emotional or physical relationship with someone. People who experience it do not consciously want to avoid intimacy; they even long for closeness, but they frequently push others away and may even sabotage relationships for many reasons.

The fear of intimacy is separate from the fear of vulnerability, though both of them can be closely intertwined. A person who has a fear of intimacy may be comfortable becoming vulnerable and showing their true self to their trusted friends and relatives. This problem often begins when a person finds relationships becoming too close or intimate. Fear of intimacy can stem from several causes. Overcoming this fear and anxiety can take time, but you can work on it if you know the signs of why you have the fear in the first place.

1. Fear Of Commitment

A person who has a fear of intimacy can interact well with others initially. It's when the relationship and its value grow closer that everything starts to fall apart. Instead of connecting with your partner on an intimate level, you find ways and excuses to end the relationship and replace it with yet another superficial relationship. Some might even call you a 'serial dater,' as you tend to lose interest after a few dates and abruptly end the relationship. The pattern of emerging short-term relationships and having a 'commitment phobia' can signify that you fear intimacy.

2. Perfectionism

The idea of erfectionism often works to push others away rather than draw them near. The underlying fear of intimacy often lies in a person who thinks he does not deserve to be loved and supported. The constant need for someone to prove themself to be perfect and lovable can cause people to drift apart from them. Absolute perfectionism lies in being imperfect. We should be able to accept the flaws of others and should expect them to do the same for us. There's no beauty in trying to be perfect when we know we cannot achieve it.

3. Difficulty Expressing Needs

A person who has a fear of intimacy may have significant difficulty in expressing needs and wishes. This may stem from feeling undeserving of another's support. You need to understand that people cannot simply 'mind read,' they cannot know your needs by just looking at you; this might cause you to think that your needs go unfulfilled and your feelings of unworthiness are confirmed. This can lead to a vicious cycle of you not being vocal about your needs and lacking trust in your partner, and your relationship is meant to doom sooner or later.

4. Sabotaging Relationships

People who have a fear of intimacy may sabotage their relationship in many ways. You might get insecure, act suspicious, and accuse your partner of something that hasn't actually occurred. It can also take the form of nitpicking and being very critical of a partner. Your trust in your partner would lack day by day, and you would find yourself drifting apart from them.

5. Difficulties with Physical Contact

Fear of intimacy can lead to extremes when it comes to physical contact. It would swing between having a constant need for physical contact or avoiding it entirely. You might be inattentive to your partner's needs and solely concentrate on your own need for sexual release or gratification. People with a fear of intimacy may also recoil from sex altogether. Both ends of the spectrum lead to an inability to let go or communicate intimately emotionally. Letting yourself be emotionally naked and bringing up your fears and insecurities to your partner may help you overcome this problem.

6. You're Angry - A Lot

One way that the deep, subconscious fear of intimacy can manifest is via anger. Constant explosions of anger might indicate immaturity, and immature people are not able to form intimate relationships. Everyone gets angry sometimes, and it's an emotion that we cannot ignore, even if we want to. But if you find that your feelings of anger bubble up constantly or inappropriately, a fear of intimacy may be lurking underneath. Don't deny these intimacy issues, but instead put them on the table and communicate effectively with the person you are interested in.

Conclusion

Actions that root out in fear of intimacy only perpetuate the concern. With effort, especially a good therapist, many people have overcome this fear and developed the understanding and tools needed to create a long-term intimate relationship.

Chapter 28:

A Guided Journal For Anxiety

Anxiety Is The Silent Killer

Anxiety is a state of worry when you are unsure about the next step. Very few people know how to handle anxiety when they face it. Instead, they bury their heads in the sand and hope that things will eventually work themselves out.

What remains unclear are the disastrous results of actions resulting from anxiety. Healthy relationships have collapsed when partners succumbed to anxiety, job opportunities have been lost, and once-in-a-lifetime chances have slipped from our hands because we were unable to contain the anxiety that was building in us.

We will lose count of the much that anxiety has cost us. Sometimes, it has been misconstrued as a "normal" feeling and nothing is done to tame it. That is the moment the rain starts beating us. Nothing much can be done when we realize the damage anxiety has done in our lives.

Here is a guided journal for anxiety:

1. Take A Step Back

Sometimes we are anxious because we do not understand what we are into. We get nervous about new experiences and do not know how to proceed from there. Our judgment is often clouded when we are in unfamiliar territories. The fear of not being right builds anxiety in us and we want to please everybody. What a herculean task!

Take a step back to get the bigger picture. This will bring clarity because you can look at all variables at once and weigh them, one after another. Moving back gives you a sense of power and control when you realize it was not that difficult in the first place. You will be more comfortable in an environment you can manipulate.

Anxiety results from the fear of the unknown. When you withdraw a little from a situation, you can comfortably evaluate it because nobody will judge you.

2. Take Off Your Mind From The Subject Matter

This is an evasion strategy. You are not always required to face your fears immediately. It is okay to withdraw your attention when you are anxious about something or an unprecedented condition. You will live to tackle it another day. Do not pressure yourself to act within a deadline. The timeframes you confine yourself within will haunt you especially when you feel inadequate for what is ahead of you.

Put your mind on things that bring you solace and calm to fight the anxiety. You understand yourself better than anyone does and you are best placed to make this decision. Think about your dream car – Rolls-Royce, Ferrari, Porsche, Chevrolet, or any other that fascinates you. Relaxing thoughts will calm you down and kick away anxiety.
Our comfort zones give us confidence because we can handle ourselves better in them. Anxiety cannot win the battle when we are in them.

3. Do Not Think Of Any Consequences – There Are None

There are no consequences of acting right. What gives anxiety room to thrive is the fear of consequences that will befall us if we do not act expectedly. Deny anxiety the pleasure of tormenting you by not accepting liability for doing the right thing.

Even in situations that present a dilemma, choose to do the right thing over the popular choice. Populism is not always right and its consequences are unavoidable. They will finally come to haunt you. To be safe, make the right choice whose consequences are positive and will bring you honor.

Regardless of how quickly you will want to work on your anxiety and make a popular choice, its results are indelible. Purpose to cure anxiety through the right channel with positive consequences.

4. Consult Widely

Consultations are the preserve of the wise. Only the wise accept that they do not have a monopoly of ideas. They seek the opinions of other people who could have had a similar experience. When you find yourself in a compromising situation, remember that you are not the first person to experience the same. Someone else has been there and they made it.

Anxiety grows in ignorance. You get nervous because you do not know how to handle the challenge your way. Seek the advice of experienced people and they will guide you on how to navigate unchartered territories. In conclusion, anyone could be anxious. What makes the difference is how different people handle it. Some turn it into an opportunity for growth while others allow it to kill their dreams. Make the right choice.

Chapter 29:

4 Ways To Make A Guy Chase You

It is normal for guys to chase after women. This is because men are hardwired to chase whatever they desire. There are moments when you will come across a man you love and desire and you'd like him to chase after you. What do you do if the guy doesn't show interest in you? For some women, they will not have a problem chasing after dudes and will always take the lead in such circumstances. Some men can be turned off by this behaviour. This is particularly because men enjoy doing the chase themselves. The moment a woman throws herself at him, it means he won't have much to do. If you want to make a guy chase after you, there are several tricks that you can use.

1. Show Confidence

Confidence is one of the greatest traits that any woman should have. When you exude confidence it will be easy to grab the attention of a man. Once he gets intrigued, he will be drawn to you. Once you believe that you are a great catch, the man will also believe the same. He will know that if he doesn't treat you well, you will leave him you for the right man. One fact that you need to know is that men love women who have confidence. This also applies to women. Whenever a confident person comes into a room, you will always find yourself looking at them. Your goal is to draw his attention and there is no better way to do that than exuding confidence. Once you appear confidence, it will look as if you are not only interested in a man and this will make the guy desire you more.

2. Keep Yourself Busy

If you want to make the guy start chasing you, you must stop making yourself available to him or you will make him feel special. He will be left guessing who or what keeps you occupied. You will not want your crush to feel so special that your universe seems to revolve around him. Therefore, use this time to do the things that have always excited you like going to the beach or enjoying your hobbies. Ensure that you avoid getting bored at all costs as this is what will cause you to miss him and reach out to him. When you have a life to enjoy, you will be contented with seeing him only once in a while and this will ensure that your relationship with him remains fresh. The longer the period that you stay away from him, the more he is going to miss you.

3. Spend Time With Your Friends

A common mistake that ladies make is to focus on their relationship too much and forget to spend time with their friends. This shouldn't be the case as it only causes the guy to feel self-important. A good idea is to schedule one night a week for going out with your girls, no matter the kind of relationship you are in. This will go a long way in helping you maintain your friendships before he came into the picture. When things don't go according to your expectations in the relationship, your friends will be the ones you turn to for advice on the next move to make. By alienating your friends, you will be showing them that they no longer matter to you. On the other hand, you will be showing your guy how special he is. You can be assured that this is bound to backfire on you and he will begin to treat you badly as he is aware that you will never leave him. It is advisable to split your time between the guy and your girl friends. This will send a message to him that your girlfriends are irreplaceable. Chances are that the guy you are eyeing also has friends with whom he goes out with at night too. The moment you alienate your friends for him, you will make him start feeling special and arrogant.

4. Have Your Own Personal Space To Make The Guy Chase You

At times, we get into a relationship and immediately make the man occupy every space in our lives. We keep thinking about where the guy is, what he is doing and with whom. You need to remember that even before he came into your life, you already had your own life. When you become needy and clingy, this may end up killing attraction as he'll feel either suffocated by your attention, or his ego will inflate and he'll become overly confident. While there is nothing wrong with showing a man that you are committed to him, when you do this in the extreme, it will only serve to make him feel extra important. Let the guy give you space for shopping and engaging in your favourite activities. This will show him that you are independent.

Chapter 30:

10 Ways To Deal With Breakup

Even if your relationship wasn't going well and the thread was on the edge of breaking, ending it all can be very hard and hurtful. It can be even more hard when you gave it all and thought that things were going smoothly from your side, but your partner disagreed and wanted to cut everything off. Wallowing in grief can be a normal phase after a breakup, but it's high time that you get over it and come back to normalcy. Here are some ways you can deal with breakup.

1. Remove Them From All Social Sites

If you're thinking of going on a complete social media fast after your breakup, it might be a good thing for you. But if not, consider removing them from all of your social media. Even if the split was amicable, seeing them might renew a twinge of sadness in your heart. You don't want to see their new love interest or how they're enjoying their lives without you.

2. Reconsider Staying Friends

As much as your heart and brain try to convince you to stay friends with them after breaking it off, it's always a bad idea. Maybe you both can be friends later on, but immediately? A big no! It will be way more hurtful and awkward to see them every day and share a bond as friends only when you both know that bond was much stronger before. Seeing each other will only make it worse for both of you to move on.

3. Call Some Friends

The worst thing you can do to yourself after a breakup is isolating yourself from the world. This would lead to you overthinking about your mistakes and would lead to bad decisions. It would cripple your mental health, and you will find yourself in a never-ending guilt loop. Instead, call your friends, hang out with them, talk to them and cry to them. Laughing with your friends is the best therapy that you can easily afford. You will feel much better with having someone around.

4. Stop Blaming Yourself

Get yourself out of the mentality of "i could've done this instead" or "i could've done that instead." if the relationship was bound to fall off, there was absolutely nothing you could have done or said that would have saved it. A relationship always requires the efforts of two; if you have put enough measures or didn't put much, then the two of you weren't a good fit.

5. Take A Break

If the relationship was all mushy and long-term, or you had a messy breakup, now will be the perfect time to take some break from dating. As much as you would feel pressured and in need of starting something new soon, you might be carrying a lot of unattended emotional baggage that you need to settle down before taking a step ahead.

6. Don't Dwell On Fixing The Relationship

It is just so much you can do to save the relationship. And once it's gone, consider it gone. Scheming and plotting on getting back with your ex would ruin your mental health. Instead, try to start focusing on yourself and your mental health. Improve your lifestyle and let bygones be bygones.

7. Eat Healthily And Exercise

Binge eating in this time of sadness is fine if it's short-term. But if you keep nibbling on junk food, it'll ruin your physical health as much as your mental health. Not having proper nutrition will leave you more stressed out as you won't be having the essentials to deal with stress. Abandon your sadness and indulge in eating healthy, and work out more to gain mental peace.

8. Get Enough Sleep

If you force yourself to stay up late at night, anxiety or sadness may overwhelm you and keep you from sleeping. It would be best if you had a proper sleep to keep yourself functional and stable. Pen down any negative thoughts you have and let them flow away from your body to the paper.

9. Neither Ignore Nor Wallow In Your Feelings

Ignoring your feelings will eventually cause an emotional outburst that you might not even be ready for, whereas wallowing in your emotions will cause you to revisit all your memories and subconsciously hurt yourself. Instead, you must healthily deal with your feelings and move on.

10. Stop Obsessing

It's natural to keep thinking about your relationship and obsessing over it after your breakup. But after a while, you should jerk the thoughts off whenever they intrude on you. It would be best to direct yourself towards more positive and constructive ideas and healthily get over your breakup.

Conclusion

Getting over a breakup isn't easy at all. But if you prioritize yourself and your needs, you will be there more quickly than you might know.

CPSIA information can be obtained
at www.ICGtesting.com
Printed in the USA
LVHW050626270722
724473LV00012B/469